TEMPORARY MEASURES

BY THE SAME AUTHOR

In Daylight (Printed Matter Press, 1995)
Monumenta Nipponica (Saru Press, 1995)
The Painting Stick (Pine Wave Press, 2005)
From the Japanese (Isobar Press, 2013)
World Without (Isobar Press, 2015)
Seeing Sights 1968–1978 (Isobar Press, 2016)

Temporary Measures

1978–1981

Paul Rossiter

ISOBAR PRESS

First published in 2017 by

Isobar Press
Sakura 2-21-23-202, Setagaya-ku,
Tokyo 156-0053, Japan
&
14 Isokon Flats, Lawn Road,
London NW3 2XD, United Kingdom

http://isobarpress.com

ISBN 978-4-907359-21-8

Copyright © Paul Rossiter, 2017
All rights reserved.

Acknowledgements
Some of these poems have appeared in *The Font: A Literary Journal for Language Teachers* and NOON: *journal of the short poem*. Earlier versions of a few of the poems appeared in *In Daylight* (Printed Matter Press, 1995).

Note
The second printing (2019) incorporates small revisions to a number of poems, as well as including one previously unpublished poem, 'Al Fintas', on page 72.

Contents

I

The Dancer and the Dance	9
Attention	12
Nightclub Work	13
Market	14
Covent Community Garden	15
Birds of a Feather	16
Crystal	18
W. S. 1611	20
Ariel	21
Pizza Apocalittica	22
Les Saltimbanques de Westbourne Park	24
10th August 1979	26
In the Sixties	28
About a Marriage	29
Funeral	30
Seeing Kung-sun's Pupil Dance	31
Wang Wei Writes a Letter	33
Lunch Break in the Park	34
A Panel from the Cathedral Door	36
Huichol	37
The Tramp	38

II

Limeuil	41
Valley Morning	42
Husbandry	44
Greetings	46

III

Paradeisos	49
Art Pepper in London	52
Rhyme	53
Cage & Cunningham	54
Cerne Abbas	56
Empires	60
Sparrow	61
Flying	66

IV

Waking	71
Al Fintas	72
Mina Al-Ahmadi, North Pier	73
Peninsula	74
Reading Horace in Kuwait	76
In the Emirate	78
The Question of Palestine	79
Cairo	80
In the Tomb of Rameses VI	81
Palaeopaphos	82
Monastery in Cyprus	84
Meltemi	86

Notes	89

I

The Dancer and the Dance

Elizabeth Walton at the Riverside Studios

Part 1: *Preparation*

a woman in a leotard
arranges her props and speaks a word:

performance

and then another word:

preparation

she makes a repeated awkward movement
on a dais at the back of the stage

to do this over and over again, she says
until it's just right

I have, she says, *to have you watch this
even though it scares me*

is it all right, she asks
to spend your life preparing for something that has no purpose?

Part 2: *Technique*

she hangs a six-foot sheet of white paper
on the wall at the back of the stage

in front of it she does the dance of dancing
the dance of technique
a torrent of *asanas* cascading one into another
balletic runs broken by virtuoso leaps and floatings

she launches herself again and again into air
at each gravity-free juncture
she flashes us a switched-on smile

with a felt-tip marker on the sheet she draws
the stylised figure of a dancer
she stands in front of it
in the posture of Vitruvian man

a trembling begins at the tips of her fingers
spreads down her arms, engulfs her body
and throws her to the floor in spasm

she leaps to her feet
tears down the paper and crumples it

Part 3: *Dance*

a tape of fragmented sounds
of silences
of city noises
a soundtrack to which she starts to move, austerely

the sounds don't say anything
or lead anywhere
or add up to anything
they're simply there

keeping such company her body is simply there
her movements occur
in a space opened up by the soundtrack
in which she encounters and counterpoints the sounds

the dance has become its own language
no longer to be spoken of
it speaks
she calls it *A New Life*

Attention

the railway workers
cross the line
stepping

casually
over one
live rail

(turning to
each other
and talking)

and then
the other – they
do this every

day, almost
not noticing
they're doing it

carefully

Nightclub Work

She steps onto the dance floor
and turns with a beautiful

practised gesture, seasoned with
a brittle nostalgia for

how it was meant to have been:
a teenage girl's winning ways

ripening to a young bride's
untarnished expectancy.

Whose dream was it anyway,
and who is it really for,

this spell she casts on the air
with only the curve of her

body to assist her? He
leaves the men at the table,

takes hold of her, clumsily,
in his excitement, in his

drunkenness, and together
they dance on the darkened floor.

Market

one scaly two scaly three
thousands
silver shiny in orange wooden boxes

    (early morning light,
      concrete quayside, Aberdeen)

whole shoals lifted late last night
in bulging, squirming, dripping nets
    out of the cold North Sea
to drown in air

longliners
    purse seiners
        factory trawlers
somewhere soon the world's last herring
is hiding in a hole at the bottom of the sea

      fish eye
      fish bone

      fish finger

unlike us
they have no eyelids

Covent Community Garden

a green place deep in a socket
where a building has been pulled like a tooth

where earth, brought in by truckloads,
is cared for under this sign:

> TO BE REDEVELOPED:
> 300,000 SQUARE FEET
> OF OFFICE SPACE

bumpy squares of threadbare turf,
pansies, tulips and forget-me-nots

a loud bee in an acoustic foxglove
beside a stack of ruined brickwork

a thrush's song beneath grey skies

a tranquillity
a made space among the
      shifting concrete pack-ice slabs
of property and finance

*'we work in the garden
as if it was going to be here forever –*

      there is no other way'

CRYSTAL

for Ursula

you showed me in the London street –
    among pneumatic drills,
      torn-up tarmac, traffic cones –
the crystal dangling from your key-ring,
preserver of sanity, you said

blue   yellow   purple   green

and suddenly a memory:

    the long lonely glen
    the great silence

blue sky, scattered clouds
tough grass and knotted heather

    cloud shadows flow
    across the mountains' flanks

    peat-stained water tumbles
    down a staircase of uneven stone

    deer feed
    high on Ben Alder's shoulder

    an eagle soars and glides

at Beallach Dubh (black pass)
    boot-soles whisper to dark earth
in windless peat-hag corridors

green mountains, purple heather,
blue sky and glinting yellow water

    intersecting planes of light

a green glen
        preserver of sanity
carried
through a world of broken paving stones

Birds of a Feather

1

shoveller   tufted duck   pochard   widgeon   coot

flute and dabble in the lake

on the web-trodden bank
a mallard stands with dignity on one leg

a moorhen steps meticulously over grass blades

2

the biography of a feather:

genetic fermentation in an albumen enclosure
a cracking open to light and air
fluff grows sleek on a plump and muscled body
a quill works loose from its socket
a shedding
a wind-quickened drift amongst shivering wavelets

soon to be mulch
soon to be less than that

3

the rotund goose
steps down the sloping bank
on its big orange feet

then topples forward to
breast the wetness, launching itself

    into the spreading ripples of
    this glimpse, this moment of entering

the wetly sensuous world of the water
the impermeable gooseness of the goose

W. S. 1611

each word
a pebble seen through water

talismanic
the isle is full of noises
liquid clarity of hallucination

'characters'
      the machinery of the stage –
to work like a carpenter at odds with
barely adequate materials

      to fly
      to swim
      to dive into the fire
      to ride on the curled clouds

that when I waked I cried to dream again

a lifetime in
      the conjurer's profession
his dreaming eye is wide open

the baseless fabric of this vision

ARIEL

active   mobile   piercing

prompt in learning or perception

the sensitive parts, esp. under the fingernails
the tenderest feelings

        quick-born
        quick-change
        quick-eyed
        quick-fire
        quick-scented
        quick-sighted
        quick-silver
        quick-witted

Old Norse   *kvikr*
Old English   *cwic*

    living

my dainty Ariel: I shall miss thee

Pizza Apocalittica

I eat my pizza in a cave at the base of a concrete cliff
Wine glasses glow on tablecloths like votive lamps
The room brims with a hundred overlapping voices
The waiters come and go like shuttles on a weaving frame
Pizzas arrive on tables (service is not included)
Edible flowers in a tapestry of wine, white linen, and bonhomie

The chef labours at his forge
Slaps out dough on his marble-topped anvil
Stokes the furnace which drives this merry-go-round
This Catherine wheel
This warped rock 'n' roll revolving in the cave of a neon-lit jukebox

It's warm tonight
But the air-conditioner is an open doorway
Feeding us a stream of Arctic tundra prehistoric air

And suddenly I find myself transported
To a chilly place of huge horizons
I look around, I'm surprised to be here
But no more surprised than anyone else
The chef, the waiters, the pizza-eaters interrupted in mid-mouthful
All clothed now in sheepskins and snug leather caps with woollen
    earflaps
And seated astride lean fierce horses with twitching flanks

But we get used to it
Our exclamations fade with our breath on the frosty air
We fall silent, we become expectant, we start to understand
We've been brought here for something momentous
Something that will declare itself in these frozen wastes
Where pools of blood in the snow look like flowers
Look much like pizzas on a tundra-sized tablecloth

We wait
We listen to the wind
We've sharpened our knives and edged our wits
We've honed our hunger to an asceticism so acute
That we can chop down skyscrapers just by thinking about it
At any moment now we'll sweep down
To take our places at the tables we reserved
By planting a seed in a telephone five thousand years ago

And at that moment
Every telephone in the world will ring
And a strangely familiar voice will announce
In a language no one has heard before but anyone can understand
That a cast of billions has been assembled, that now we can
      bring you
At great expense and all the way from nowhere
The greatest show on earth, it will last for one-tenth of a second

Les Saltimbanques de Westbourne Park

I cycle uphill in the dark
Beneath the tower block with the searchlight in its forehead
Past the construction site grinding its teeth under floodlights
Under the belly of the concrete motorway centipede

Then up to the crest of the hill
And the iron bridge over the old canal
A placid curve of water singing
Forgotten nineteenth-century songs under its damp breath

Tonight a crowd has assembled on the bridge
Others have gathered on the towpath below
As I arrive there's an explosion –
A bomb! is it a bomb? no, it's a firework

We peer across the water to
A commotion being enacted in a derelict back garden
Mysterious figures trying by torchlight
To lift a large, black vinyl ball out of dark water

Oh, it's a what-d'you-call-it, a community festival
Torches burn, the water runs gold, red and black
The crowd are like bees trying to remember
Something they once heard about flowers

A van with dented panels swerves to a halt by the curb
Two young black guys jump out
One wears stone-washed jeans and a T-shirt taut over bulging
    muscles
The other, shades and a floppy hat at the hippest possible angle

A police car crawls towards us and gives us all a stare
Probes for misdemeanours with its headlights
Suddenly its radio crackles, tyres squeal, blue lights flash
The siren fades from earshot, life goes on

A loudspeaker clears its throat and a voice announces
That Thanks to Our Patient Participation in Today's Events
The End of the World
Has Been Postponed for a Few More Weeks

The voice is tired
Tired with being an underpaid social policy graduate in 1979
Tired with the friction between the word *patient*
And the word *participation*

A smattering of applause
A small shower on a summer night
Nomads camped out on a bomb site
Uncertain celebrations

City of rotten molars

10th August 1979

cycling Great Western Road on my way to Fulham
I see a woman in a sari
waiting for a bus by a scaffolded building
and suddenly I'm in Calcutta

    coriander, cow-dung, charcoal smoke,
    dust stained red with squirts of betel juice,
    drinking hot sweet tea
    from a small cup made of earth

I wish I really were in West Bengal, but by now
I'm cycling down the North End Road

    electrical goods, wet fish shops
    bookmakers, discount clothing stores
    the street market in full vociferous cry
    squshd vgtbls in the gutters

chain the bike to a lamp post
go into the new flat to get the electricity connected
the task completed by an aging actor
who does this kind of thing when he's resting

    terrible, dear, thank you for asking,
    I've just broken my top set –
    and my first recording for months to do tonight –
    yes, that's right – SW6, *spelt* T-H-I-X

a spare key from the landlord in his butcher's shop
ruddy-faced emperor of a white-tiled pandemonium

blood-stained aprons, shouts of the lads
cleavers whack on chopping blocks
sides of beef sway on stainless steel hooks

even the stink of blood doesn't dismay me today
life is good, and anything is welcome to a place in this poem

on a hoarding across the street a Polo Mint ad tells me:

nothing is a patch on a hole in your pocket

In the Sixties

she was nineteen
he was twenty-three

a very beautiful boy, she said
first a pop star and then a photographer

eating pistachio nuts one night
not long after they'd met
one of her teeth suddenly crumbled to dust

>she'd just given birth
>calcium low
>gone to make the baby's bones

two days later he left:

can't be having a bird whose teeth fall out

About a Marriage

for Jane

a Sunday drive
just the two of them
she driving
he beside her reading the map

his intense fragility, she thought, *his distance*

nothing to say to each other now without the kids
as they drove through mist
to a place where
had there been no mist

they could have seen half the hills of England

Funeral

what exactly was inside that box
heaped with flowers

impossible
it should have been a person

and I had never known such absence

yet could not think of
his body as an it

no way to speak
or treat with such precision
of nothingness

ceremony without consolation
grey skies
the yew trees guttering in the wind

Seeing Kung-sun's Pupil Dance

On 15 November 767 I saw Li-shih-er-niang dance at the house of Yuan Ch'ih, Lieutenant-Governor of K'uei province. She so impressed me that I asked her who she'd trained with, and she told me she'd been Kung-sun's pupil.

I remember seeing Kung-sun dance at Yen-ch'eng fifty years ago, when I was only a boy. The purity of her style and her incisive attack were unrivalled – no one during the early part of the Emperor's reign, before the Disturbances, understood dance as she did. Her face like jade, her brocade dress ... but I'm white-haired now, and even her pupil is past her prime.

Some years ago, Zhang Xu, the master of the grass-writing style of calligraphy, often saw Kung-sun dance at Yeh-tsien. The result, which delighted him, was that he found his calligraphy greatly improved – which tells you something about the sort of person Kung-sun was.

    years ago Kung-sun astonished the world
    watchers gathered around
    like range beyond range of bewildered hills
    and when she left the stage
    heaven and earth danced on and on

    she was nine suns falling out of the sky
    she was dragons soaring through space
    her entrance was a thunderclap
    her stillness green ice and winter light

    red lips
    sleeves embroidered with pearls
    ashes and silence

but Li-shih has caught up the fragrance
and the old mastery haunts her dance

among the Emperor's eight thousand dancers
Kung-sun knew no equal –
fifty years turn over like the flick of a hand
dust clouds
dark winds on the palace for fifty years

the Pear Garden dancers are gone like mist
and Li-shih's face as she dances
      is like the sun in winter
saplings planted by the Emperor's tomb
have joined hands above the pathway
grass withers on the walls of set stone

the mats are edged with tortoise shell
the urgent flutes
      fade to stillness again
at the height of pleasure comes sorrow
the moon begins its climb in the east

I am an old man
my future a tangle of mountains

my feet get weary of the path

after Tu Fu

Wang Wei Writes a Letter

February
clear bright weather

last night I climbed Hua-tzu Hill –
full moon on all the country
the waters of the Wang River
      rippling in its light
distant lanterns coming and going
      in cold hills beyond the woods
dogs barking in lanes
      sounding like leopards
the pounding of grain in the village
heard between strokes of a distant bell

we must wait for the spring:
trees, green grass, green hills
steep paths beside clear streams
dace leaping out of the water
gulls soaring
dew wet on the grassy banks
the morning call of pheasants in the corn

all this will be with us soon
surely then we can go walking together?

no urgency

this comes to you by a hillman
from Wang Wei
man of the hills

Lunch Break in the Park

The greylag has been re-established by releasing birds in suitable areas, but the resulting flocks in southern Britain tend to be semi-tame, and to lack the special appeal of the truly wild geese to be found in Scotland.

1

the sky a jubilation of winter blue
and a wind so cold it hurts

beside the pond
an old woman scatters bread
to a squabble of ducks and burly geese
that seethe around her shoes and knees

an avenue of bare branches
      leads the eye to a chilly horizon
a line of office blocks
as remote and blank as an Arctic cliff

2

the pond is a zero of dazzling blue and white
with ice-shards tinkling at its edges

five nodding greylags circulate
      then come ashore and preen
snaking their necks backwards
wriggling their bills in amongst their feathers

a conclave of muscular dwarfs in tight brown suits
meticulously checking their pockets

3

heading back towards the gate
past the silent bandstand

> (curlicues, scrollwork, flutings –
> a toy left out on a frosty lawn)

when suddenly:

ragged trumpeting calls
extended necks and gaping orange bills
the clap of heavy wings
as a flight of greylags slams past just overhead

I walk back to my Kensington desk
through a northern landscape
of wintry moor and frozen marshland

> ears ringing

with hoarse goose music and
the aftershock of wings

A Panel from the Cathedral Door

Hildesheim, AD 1015

Old Man God
        points
a wrathful finger

at the man who points
at the woman who points
at the serpent
        curled
at the foot of the tree
of all the world. What

        twist in the psyche
        brought forth dirt? The man

and the woman crouch
like strange beasts in the field
more abject than any beasts, as abject as

        some fearful adolescent
        whimpering at his prayer stool

in the field of all the world

where the goodman, the goodwoman
cringe
and try to hide their nakedness

        from that old man and his
        indignant finger –

him with The Book in his other hand.

Huichol

masks
stone carvings
shields of interwoven splints

bamboo hoops laced with yarn (full moon)
or with a single strand from side to side (new moon)

triangles of painted lath suspended from threads
tiny hunting bows ornamented with beads or yarn

embroideries on cotton
beeswax crosses embellished with coils of beads

store-bought mirrors
(cosmic openings, emergence holes of the gods)

a smoke-blackened gourd
hangs beneath the roof

(the heart of Grandfather Fire)

The Tramp

in the graveyard
said: Jesus

is coming soon
you know

I've only taken
to drink

as a temporary
measure

II

LIMEUIL

Vézère   Dordogne
that's what we called them until here

    swift over rounded pebbles
    stronger in the centre

greenbrown muscle of water

a high arched bridge over each river
a green tongue of land
reaches down between them

to touch the

    unimpedable
    unnameable

moment of meeting waters

Valley Morning

1

each morning
fog curls among trees, wood smoke drifts

there should be higher ground
above these misty pine-fledged slopes

        snowfields and naked rock
        beneath a blaze of sun

but no, no land above 500 metres hereabouts

        we live in the foothills of
        range upon range of dreams

beaded dewdrops on the eagle's feathers

2

every wooden door is open
you may knock on any one you choose

mother
        father
child and grandchild
the woodman pulls on his boots

        dog barks
        bird calls
        cock crows

first cup of coffee in the chilly dawn

this is the only life there is

Husbandry

The stream tumbles down the terraced hillside
and enters the grassy, stone-walled plot
by a small fall, and then is channelled
into a rectangular pool deep enough
for the ducks and geese to swim in.

The sides of the pond are neatly fettled:
wooden stakes support caulked planks
which keep the dark earth back.
At the pool's far end, a gap in the earthen bank
is plugged with a chipped concrete block –

a lip over which the stream continues.
A cleanly incised drainage channel leads
the water along beside the boundary wall,
so the ducks and geese have not only
a pond but also enough dry ground

to feed, preen and roost on.
At the corner of the enclosure, a section
of salvaged concrete pipe directs
the water onwards. Where the stream reaches
the stony hill path, the water tumbles

over another fall and into a channel
that leads downhill towards the river.
Here, a tin can has been wedged into a cranny,
a hosepipe attached to the bottom of it.
Most of the water continues in the stream, but

the pressure drives some into the hose
and thence into the sprinkler
in the vegetable patch across the path,
where succulent aubergines glisten in sunlight
beneath a four-foot rainbow.

When not needed, remove the can from the stream.

Greetings

In a clearing at the top of the hill
an old man is tending his vegetables,
his dog stretched out by the hedge.

He stumps back down the furrow
to greet us – *m'sieurs dames* –
a strong handshake, a glint in his eye.

*J'aime les Anglais, j'étais à Dunkerque,
quarante – plusieurs bombes!*
He mimes the bombs and laughs at them

and at his own survival.
I ask if all three plots up here are his
and he takes me to mean, does he

own all this, as far as the eye can see?
Je suis pas capitaliste! A sweep of the hand
to the far horizon, and a huge guffaw:

Mon chien, il s'appelle Milord!

III

Paradeisos

1

stone parapet
the curve of the long water

invisible shaping grammar
the human planted order
behind these self-ordered growings

various oaks
various ash and elm

paradise is not a place
but is made and kept in mind

a serenity imagined and
    projected onto earth
        excluding all division

the willows tremble at the water's brink

2

'garden' from Old English *geard*

fence   enclosure   dwelling

pairidaeza (Persian): walled garden
παράδεισος: enclosed garden
    orchard, pleasure ground

pairi: around
diz (Sanskrit *dih*): to mould, form, or shape
      (for example, a wall of earth)
from the Indo-European DHEIG: knead, mould, form
from which Latin *fingere*

figure   feign   fiction

it is planted in our tongues
the code is written in the seed

Figulus

draws the world to its lip
on the spin of his potter's wheel

3

and what is kneaded from the clay
is not the flesh

but the frontiers of our perception
a shaping grace

as now the music of this moment
this making
the shapely specificity of this world

has drawn me to the gap in the trees

       where the even turf stretches
       down to the water's edge

to drink
from this earthen cup
the fictive waters of our oldest story

Art Pepper in London

he introduces his Bulgarian pianist as

> *a man who wanted to be free in his music
> so he came over here to the USA …*

London? USA?

> and, then again, that word *free* …

B52s lined up on the runways
> *(the free world's unsinkable aircraft carrier)*
radar scanning the eastern horizon
technicians running checks in their bunkers

while in this smoky jazz club
not so far from the threatened frontier

> the floodlit wire
> the tank tracks in the dust
> the armoured phalanxes at their war games

piano and alto sax
pour freely forth their music

> in the mode of white Los Angeles
> nineteen fifty-something

in the key of cold war minor

Ronnie Scott's, 18 June 1980

Rhyme

white plastic sandals
    hare krishna
faded orange robes
    hare krishna
grey shaven skulls
    krishna krishna
other-planet eyeballs
    hare hare

    chanting and
    ching-ching-a-ling finger-
    cymballing along
    Kensington High Street

while in a boutique behind them

    bald, ash-white and ascetic, clad
    in exquisite orange-yellow robes

a window dresser's mannequins devoutly pose

Cage & Cunningham

A man sits on a folding chair at a desk with a phone.
He dials. He speaks. He listens to his speaking.
He speaks a language from another planet, one
where time is different from here. No, he doesn't,
he speaks a language-like language from here
where time is no different from now. I don't
understand what he says and I don't mind a bit.

Another man steps across the wooden floor,
slow and stiff, a bit arthritic around the pelvis.
He looks out from beneath his eyebrows.
A repeated stork-like placing of the feet.
Nothing is expressed; something happens.
Someone is looking out through his eyes.

The speaking man stops speaking. Now
he's pushing a wooden chair across the floor.
The chair cries out loud, juddering
in the stress and tremble of its frictions.
The man allows the sounds to be, he listens,
he's interested in what sounds might happen,
he allows the chair to speak its say.

He pushes a blackboard, he pushes a rake,
he pushes a bright red tubular steel trolley.
Things stripped of our meanings, now at last
they can believe in themselves. No, they can't,
they're just a blackboard, a trolley, a rake, and
I've never seen such objects before. They speak.

He pushes a grand piano across the floor.
Its casters jammed, its loud pedal held down,
it squeaks and growls and grinds, the air is filled
with giddying vistas of stacked harmonics.
It sounds like the end of the world but it isn't.
What it is really is a piano being pushed
across a wooden floor. The pushing man listens.

The moving man moves. One of his hands
wriggles and flutters in front of him.
The action is tossed to the other hand
to continue. The rest of his uneventful body
remains quite still and self-contained.

Nothing happens. Something happens.
A police car's passing siren is a sound.

Goldsmiths, University of London, 18 July 1980

Cerne Abbas

1

weapons clink in evening silence
leather creaks
a *centuria* of men from Apulia, Sicily and Provence
    in iron helmets and hob-nailed sandals
enter a green secluded valley

    corn, cattle, gold, silver and iron
    hides, slaves and clever hunting dogs
    are what they've been sent here for

the Giant faces them
tall on his hill in the low northern light,
his outline, chalk-white, incised in steep, springy turf,
ancient, with upraised club and jutting phallus

2

five hundred years on, a missionary to the Saxons,
spirit ablaze with the glory of Christ,
walks the same road, bringing news of salvation,
glad tidings of the triumph of daylight

night is coming on, but he feels his faith to be
a light militant that will defeat all darkness

the villagers pelt him with mud, tie
a cow's tail to his arse, and chase him away

washing off the filth at a nearby spring
he has a vision of God in His radiance and falls to his knees

night gathers on the downs
the Giant looms on the hill

3

came via Dorchester, turned off at Hardy's statue
then drove up the valley and parked the car

and now we walk in sunshine among cottages –
stone, half-timber, white stucco, or brick,
      flowers framing their doorways,
the downs tall and green at their backs

the Giant leans over the village
an unblinking presence

each evening, century after century,
the village has locked its doors
      against darkness and silence
and lit its small lamps against nightfall

4

sheep-cropped turf
a thorn tree high on the down
the Giant fenced off with a National Trust fence,
above his left shoulder
an iron-age earthwork on the prow of the hill

    silence
    evening light
    a whisper of wind in gorse bushes

four-square but diminutive from this distance
the church raises its tower
shepherd-like above a huddle of colloquial roofs

our car
small in the faraway car park

5

the Giant, of course, may not be pre-Roman at all
Roman perhaps
or medieval
or even later than that

    first mention:
    for repareing ye Giant 3 shillings
    (churchwarden's records, 1694)

we have a laugh –
    what a diligent, un-partisan churchwarden! –
as we get into the car,
close the doors and drive away

6

sheep-cropped turf
thorn tree high on the rounded hill

gnarled roots
deep in the chalky earth

black limbs stir
in the wind off the downs

green leaves
catching the last of the light

Empires

rice farmers, woodcutters, fishermen
saké brewers and sellers of radishes
bean-curd makers, minor feudal retainers
noodle-stall owners and mendicant priests

emerged in 1868
into a brave new world of empires

a hundred years on,
snagged in a thorn tree's branches
      beside a stony Himalayan path,
an empty Mitsubishi fertiliser sack

flips and flaps like a prayer flag
legislating in the mountain wind

Sparrow

i

I sit in sunshine in the launderette doorway
reading a paperback anthology
as I wait for the cycle to finish

planes pass overhead, one each ninety seconds
descending steadily to Heathrow
sucking kerosene from wing-tanks to feed their engines
bringing thousands each hour to their landfall

a seventeenth-century voice numbers
the kisses beyond number he wants from Celia:

> *adde a thousand, and so more*
> *till you equall with the store*
> *all the grasse that Rumney yeelds*
> *or the sands in Chelsey fields*

Catullus Englished
the Libyan desert transposed
to lush Kentish pasture and Chelsea's pebbled shore

a few pages more, a hundred years on:

> *this casket* India's glowing Gems unlocks
> *and all* Arabia *breathes from yonder Box*

a different leaf
      from the Roman codex
some bankable new lines in imported goods

(in the Directors' Court Room
at East India House on Leadenhall Street
a bas-relief: *Britannia Receiving the Riches of the East*)

some pages more, another hundred years:

measure the course of that sulphur orb that lights the darksom day
set stations on this breeding Earth & let us buy and sell

2

    … till you match each brick and tile
    in Lots Road's tow'ring chimneyed pile
    (near where the Thames doth ebb and flood
    o'er Chelsea Creek's sour sheeted mud),
    or all the coal therein devoured
    so London Transport may be powered;
    or the yield of cash-quick crops
    that superseded Romney's flocks,
    where now the shielded Magnox core
    affrights poor Dungeness's shore …

3

*The aircraft is of wide-fuselage, low-wing design with four podded under-wing turbofan engines, developing between 264 and 276*kN *of thrust. The fuel tanks are in the wings and the tail-plane, with reserve fuel tanks in the outer wing sections. The maximum fuel capacity is* 216,840 *litres.*

Its maximum takeoff weight is 333,400 kilograms, and it has a cruise speed of about 900 kph, and a range of up to 7,200 nautical miles. On a flight of 3,500 miles carrying 56,700 kilograms of fuel, it will consume an average of five gallons (19 litres) per mile.

4

round-hulled, single-masted,
        square-sailed, double-ruddered vessels
ride at anchor off the port of Ostia

    blessed Plenty pours her brimming horn

from Egypt: wheat, marble, ivory and slaves
from Britain: tin, lead, pigs and oak
from Spain: gold, silver, copper, fish-paste, olive oil and wine

    blessed Plenty pours her brimming horn

seventeen hundred years
and the vernal gale fills the swelling sail
    of an Indiaman rounding the Cape
(cotton, silk, linen, indigo, saltpetre, tea)

    blessed Plenty pours her brimming horn

and now at Heathrow, Jumbos
    long-haul from margins to metropolis
disgorge stacked pallets
onto oil-stained concrete and asphalt aprons

    blessed Plenty pours her brimming horn

and emerging from First Class at Terminal Three
to the bows and smiles of the flight attendants

> *blessed Plenty pours her brimming horn*

our new accountants of unquenchable desire
men in expensive shoes
whose briefcases hold the future

5

young William Blake,
walking south one day to Dulwich, saw
a mulberry tree
with *bright angelic wings bespangling every bough like stars*

> angels on Peckham Rye?
> who might see those now?

alabaster skin, faint blue stains below her eyes,
a young girl runs and skips in sunshine
on the pavement outside the launderette

and she coughs from time to time,
and it's bronchial,
comes from deep inside her body's smallness

> (the planes pass overhead, one
> each ninety seconds,
> descending steadily to Heathrow)

in the forecourt of the adjacent house –
home to five cracked flower pots,
three dustbins and a struggling tree –

a quick-eyed sparrow, all feathers and brio,
swerves in flight and
lands on a branch with a *cheep*

7 August 1980

FLYING

> *nil mortalibus ardui est* (Horace, *Odes* 1.3)

we sit in rows in a vibrating aluminium tube
Muzak wafts from speakers to sugar our anxiety
the hatches are sealed shut
> *doors to automatic please*
we're about to be projected by kerosene into very thin air

we turn onto the runway, and power
is slipped from its leash

> *we're all in this together*

Greeks setting keel to breakers, Phoenicians
putting out across the elemental sea

brass pots, swords and ploughshares
> cantilever spans and Rolls-Royce engines
we delve in the world and wrench it to our purposes
the Tibetans were right
when they made their blacksmiths outcasts

> but: *we're all in this together,* and
> there's no way out except one

and so in the end one says *yes!*
and arrives at 30,000 feet
exulting despite oneself in the twentieth century

after lunch, Anatolia:

> wrinkled sun-burnt hills,
> tiny cross-hatched fields in folded valleys

and a fierce blue lake
staring up from inside its rim of crusted salt
at our sliver of edged metal
flying far too high to cast a shadow

1 *September* 1980

IV

Waking

the window of blank awakening

    the pattern holds good
    weeds spring up on the sill

the unanswerable landscape reassembles
in an instant
to what we always knew

and we go down
from the empty places, to walk

    the ruined valleys, inhabit
    the abrasive cities

delight despite ourselves
with only naked consciousness to clothe us

Al Fintas

a breeze-block café under the stars
somewhere to eat on the edge of a desert
cooking smells drift through the warm night air

paraffin lamps placed on earth out front
red carpets spread in dust
so men in dishdashas may recline on cushions
sip smoke from bubbling hookahs

the owner comes out of his kitchen, bearing
a glowing lump of charcoal held in tongs,
moves to and fro like a night nurse
tending the pipes of his patients

> a hospice for an old dispensation
> lingering here a little longer yet

twenty yards away
behind a shimmering wire-mesh fence
the six-lane highway floods past, headlights glaring

Mina al Ahmadi, North Pier

who could doubt the solid funded presence
    here where the Company extends
its steel spider-work out to sea
to feed the restless queue of tankers

but the swallows
    the green taste of Europe still upon them
passing through in swift lilting flight
above hot sand and tidemark

heartbeat
    under feathers
the small precisely navigating brain
behind each pair of small black eyes

messengers who
    arouse the doubt that
saves us, who bring us back to
our senses

to sandbanks and spits
    to the little clusters of offshore rocks
all recent superstructures
tentative again

Peninsula

> *Qasr as Sabiyah, Kuwait, 1980*

camels graze
on ochre-yellow desert below
an escarpment of fractured sandstone

Bedouin tents in the distance
air-conditioners bolted to their tent-poles
pick-up trucks parked outside them

wind and sun, silence
except for the faint throb of generators
intermittent on the breeze

some miles further, no more tents
just a desert with a road running through it
wisps of sand blowing across its tarmac

and then at journey's end a white building:
the expensive road came all these miles
to a concrete box with a policeman in it

to a beach of banked white seashells
to the rusting carcase of a ship
on an empty foreshore

where shoals of mudskippers
skitter across the tidal flats
with startled eyes and popping mouths

where buzzards perch on grass-tufts
unmoving, unblinking,
bolts of lightning gloved in feathers

where, if you listen carefully, you can hear

the rumble of the Iraqi guns
pulverising Iranians
in the Shatt al-Arab marshlands

Reading Horace in Kuwait

> *pone sub curru nimium propinqui*
> *solis in terra domibus negata* (*Odes* 1.22)

1

brief February rains
a gun-grey sky above a suddenly half-green desert
cloud-bursts
      splashes of watery sunlight
gas-flares reel in a gusty wind

2

in a leafy glade –
      hush, soft grass and summer flowers,
an Italy drowned in rural quietness
      far from the rigours and alarms
of the empire's desert borders

      where the sun steers close and
      mile on mile is uninhabited heat –

Horace, unarmed, is wandering
outside the bounds of his Sabine farm
singing of Lalage, his *sweet chatterer*

when he meets a wolf
      (Parthia feeds no beast that size
      Africa, nurse of monsters, breeds lesser lions)
which at once turns tail

the fierce un-Roman world

> *parched Numidia or*
> *Syrtes' burning sands*

disarmed
on meeting *a good man innocent of sin*

3

twenty years before
the legions led by Crassus
      crossed the Euphrates on a bridge of boats
flights of Parthian arrows flickered through the air
and hardly a man came back

a flash flood
sluices down the wadi, runs into sand
and vanishes without a trace

In the Emirate

His Highness the Amir Jaber al-Ahmad al-Jaber al-Sabah
today visited

>heaps of sand
>roadside concrete detritus
>stacks of splintery four-foot laths

Kuwait's three famous water towers
(the largest contains a million gallons of water)

>shovels, pickaxes
>a snout-nosed yellow digger
>cheap boots and dusty overalls

which take the form of
the perfumed water-spraying equipment

>dinar wages
>saved week by week
>sent home (Yemen, Balochistan) once a quarter

used by Kuwaiti people in the past
at wedding parties and on social occasions

The Question of Palestine

on the way to Kuwait City
we drive through Hawalli, a Palestinian area

>   battered low-rise buildings
>   broken windows
>   rubbled streets, pot-holed tarmac

so *this* is where my students live ...

in English composition classes
>   in the air-conditioned training centre

the Palestinian students have just one topic
although many ways to express it:

>   olive trees, orange groves, the empty well,
>   the big iron key,
>   the deeds to the house
>   in a box under a bed in a camp in Lebanon

yesterday
Khalil apologised for an absence from class
his first son was being born

>   *congratulations, warmest congratulations!*
>   *what are you going to call him?*

Balfour, he said, looking me straight in the eye

Cairo

an avenue of palm trees
a line of dilapidated horse-drawn carriages
conservatories with shattered panes of glass –
the past now looks like this

the present is a power plant
an incessant clamour of machines
broken blackened window grilles
grimy walls lit by thirty-watt bulbs

the present is an Institute of Arabic Music
guarded by teenage conscripts
with Kalashnikovs and bayonets
disconsolate among heaped sandbags

the present is a bus terminus
a maze of darkened concrete walkways
small figures hurrying through gloom
to elbow themselves onto shuddering buses

the present is a muddy park, where rain
drips from palm trees onto stalls
selling second-hand English textbooks
marketing management medicine maths

the young men leaf through them –
the aspiration, the seriousness,
the almost impossible odds –
what futures will flow from this

In the Tomb of Rameses VI

he has had centuries to get acquainted
with the goddess on his ceiling

feet in the east, hands in the west
she gives birth to the sun each day

mother of gods, mistress of ritual
she is the river of the sky

her overarching belly is filled with stars
her breasts will sweeten nothingness

she extends her arms towards him
from the ceiling of the world

but can never reach him
here in the house of the dead

Paleopaphos

ubi amor ibi oculis est

1

a scuffed patch of mosaic in the dust
some annotated chunks of greyish stone

a small white village
    sunk in sun and silence
beyond the perimeter fence

    once the greatest
    temple of Aphrodite in the whole Greek world

to fence things off for preservation
is one method of neglect

2

nightly rituals of
the seafront disco dance floor

see! her chosen single couple

    each move
    of hand or hip or thigh
        of fingertip or foot, each
    answering glance of eye

says the sacred space is always
here
    in the dance of those who choose
to set foot within her sphere

3

    moment by moment
        arising from the world
    blown salt spray in the wind off the sea

    you break us open again and again

    he came to her bed:

        he had not thought that life
        would hold such glory for him

4

a cool insistent breeze
    comes in over the wave crests
dances
among ruffled hair at forehead and nape

    white cliffs
    a curve of bay

absence so great
it has the taste of presence

    shivering up the spine

again and again
born out of restlessness, nothingness

    the glittering sea

Monastery in Cyprus

dry friable earth
fields step down to the sea

a cloister
a small perfection of rhyming arches
a circular pool
spring-water runs over a lip of stone

    the slow flow of prayer

hidden from the world
raised by hand for the love of God
a courtyard which quietly breathes the sky
second by second
    water's silvery tinkle
the constant small inventions of peace

chapel with its friendly barrel roof
courtyard with its glancing swallows

crepuscular interior
    lit with the glint of candles
and the memory of countless small devotions

little dynamo half-buried in a hillside
little cave of darkness, icons and patriarchs

little snail, little snail-shell
creeping down the centuries

teach us
how to be insouciant, obscure and happy
teach us how

so untendentiously to maintain the sacred

Meltemi

the Aegean
grinds its teeth on a shelf of pebbles,
yachts fret at anchor in a fierce blue swell

a speedboat whines and
spatters across the bay, its clamour
gusting in and out of focus on the wind

in the new hotel, the doors
slam open and shut, the windows
rattle in their frames

> (but the road to the old village
> is hushed, a dappled
> tunnel of ancient olive trees)

after sunset we take
the zigzag path up the mountain
to naked granite, wind and darkness

where we lie on our backs
on still warm stone, and watch
the sky silt up with a million grains of starlight

notes

Notes

10th AUGUST 1979: A Polo is a hollow peppermint sweet. Advertising slogan: 'the mint with the hole'.

SEEING KUNG-SUN'S PUPIL DANCE: David Hawkes, *A Little Primer of Tu Fu* (1967). The 'Disturbances' mentioned in the introduction were the 'An-Shi Disturbances', otherwise known as the An Lu-shan Rebellion, of 755–763. David Hinton, in the biography attached to his *Selected Poems of Tu Fu* (1988), reports that the population of China fell from 53 million before the rebellion to 17 million afterwards. That is, 36 million people died, were displaced, rendered homeless, or otherwise lost to view during these few years, a figure that represents two-thirds of the population of the Chinese empire or one-sixth of the population of the world at that time.

WANG WEI WRITES A LETTER: Adapted from G. W. Robinson's translation of a prose letter from Wang Wei to P'ei Ti in his *Wang Wei: Poems* (1973).

HUICHOL: The Huichol (or Wixáritari) are Native Mexicans living in the mountains of central Mexico; they are famous for their art, which, whether made for commercial or for religious purposes, uses ancient symbols from their shamanistic, peyote-based religion.

PARADEISOS: Figulus (Latin): a potter, a maker of earthenware goods.

SPARROW: For most of the twentieth century (1905–2002) the Lots Road power station in Chelsea supplied electricity for the London Underground; in its prime it burnt 700 tonnes of coal a day. Dungeness A on Romney Marsh (1965–2006) was a generation-1 nuclear power station, producing both electricity for the national grid and plutonium-239 for the British atomic weapons programme. The refrain in part 4 is adapted from a line in James Michie's translation of Horace's *Carmen Saeculare* (17 BCE).

FLYING: *Nil mortalibus ardui est*: 'nothing is too difficult (too lofty) for humankind'.

READING HORACE IN KUWAIT: The phrases in italics are adapted from James Michie's translation of Ode 1.22 in *The Odes of Horace* (1963); the epigraph is translated in the first quotation in part 2.

PALEOPAPHOS: Paleopaphos ('Old Paphos'), the birthplace of Aphrodite, is a few miles along the coast from the modern town of Paphos. *Ubi amor ibi oculus est:* 'where there is love, there is sight' (Richard of St Victor). The quotation in part 3 is from Book III of *The Odyssey.*

MELTEMI: A strong, dry wind from the north that blows in the Aegean in summer.

www.ingramcontent.com/pod-product-compliance
Lightning Source LLC
Chambersburg PA
CBHW031206090426
42736CB00009B/801